THE

Acts of Pilate (Acta Filati)

IMPORTANT TESTIMONY OF PONTIUS PILATE,
RECENTLY DISCOVERED,

BEING HIS OFFICIAL REPORT TO THE EMPEROR TIBERIUS,
CONCERNING THE

CRUCIFIXION OF CHRIST.

———

EDITED BY
REV. GEO. SLUTER, A. M.,
Late Secretary Missions, Presbyterian Synod of Missouri.

————

SOLD ONLY BY SUBSCRIPTION.

————

SHELBYVILLE, IND.:
M. B. ROBINS, PUBLISHER AND PRINTER.
1879.

TO ALL
who love the Truth,
search after it,
and are willing to abide by it,
Catholic or Protestant,
within or without the Church, —
with the earnest hope that it may lead to a
deep and true devotion to Jesus,
This Contribution
to the Historical Evidence for the Divine Origin of
Christianity, is respectfully

Dedicated
by

THE EDITOR.

"This is the religious question of the age. We rejoice in it, and thank the infidel biographers of Jesus for having urged it upon the world."

PHILIP SCHAFF, D. D.

PREFACE.

My object in publishing this book is to show that the historic evidence for the history contained in the Gospels is ample and explicit. If unbelievers demand heathen testimony concerning the origin of Christianity, here it is in abundance, and of the clearest kind. By glancing through the Table of Contents it will be seen, that the testimony of the Roman procurator is here surrounded by many great writers of remote antiquity. I could have given still more, but these will suffice to show how full is the Historic Evidence for Christianity.

It may perhaps be necessary to guard the reader against supposing this to be the spurious or forged Acta, to which allusion is made by many writers.

The best and most complete edition of these is that of Fabricius (Codex Apocryphus, Edition 1703). A full and accurate literal translation may be found in the 19th volume of the Ante-Nicene Library, published by T. & T. Clark. Edinburgh, 1870. They are certainly spurious, and the inventions of a later day. They are full of absurdities and almost utterly unworthy of respect. But the Vatican copy, which I here present, is an entirely different paper. I have carefully examined the Acta Paradosis, Mors, and Epistolae Pilati, both in the Latin and Greek forms, and I assure the reader there is not a line or trace of similarity between them and this document. It will speak for itself. I think the internal evidence is such as cannot fail to produce conviction upon careful examination. The very fact that it does not give anything new or singular is in favor of its genuinenes s. In this it differs entirely from the contents of the Apocryphal writings. It is interesting also to notice the statement of Pilate, that he trembled, when Jesus for the first time entered his presence—why did he tremble? There was good reason for it. He was in the presence of the Son of God. Among the internal evidences of its genuineness I cannot refrain from calling special attention to what Pilate says of the Resurrection. He does not say that Jesus arose from the dead, but that his tomb was found empty.

The style proves it to be the true Acta. It is not in the corrupt Latin of the Apocryphal Acta Paradosis, Mors, and Epistolæ, but in the pure and glowing rhetoric of the Classic period of Roman Literature.

The discovery of this long lost testimony of Pilate, amid the vast mass of unedited parchments in the Vatican, is certainly an event of extraordinary importance in the history of the Christian Evidences.

I would suggest to the reader, to study the text of the Acta in the light and with the aid of the Historical and Critical Notes. They contain matter necessary to be understood, and will richly repay careful perusal. Indeed, they are essential to the completeness of the impression to be produced by the book.

Its preparation has been a source of great pleasure and satisfaction to me, and that it may prove of advantage to others, is my sincere and earnest desire.

G. S.

SHELBYVILLE, INDIANA,
September, 1879.

CONTENTS.

INTRODUCTION

HOW THE EDITOR CAME INTO POSSESSION OF THE DOCUMENT.

The following remarkable document, like many other invaluable parchments that have never been published to the world, has, until now, been literally concealed among the twenty-four thousand manuscripts in the penetralia of the Vatican. Its existence, from the earliest periods of the Christian Era, is familiar to men of letters. References to it abound in all profound works concerning the historical aspects of the argument for the divine origin of Christianity; e. g. Lardner, Horne, Kitto, Farrar, Andrews, and Tischendorf.

Many have supposed that the document had, in the course of ages, been lost. But as the Sinaitic manuscript of the New Testament was concealed from the world until 1844, when it was brought to light by the indefatigable zeal of Dr. Constantine Tischendorf,— so, strange to say, this important testimony to Christ, was not accessible until about twenty years ago. A learned man of Germany, not a Theologian, spent some five years in Rome, consulting the library of the Vatican. He became well acquainted with the chief custodian, and enjoyed unusual liberties. He finally gained access even to the ancient Manuscripts — the most valuable collection in the world, embracing one of the oldest codices of the Bible. To his surprise and pleasure he came upon a collection called the Emperor Tiberius Cæsar's (hurt; and among the strange and curious state papers here deposited, he happened upon the famous official report of the Prefect, Pontius Pilate, concerning the Trial and Crucifixion of Christ.

As he was not personally interested in Theological studies, the subject passed from his mind. But some years afterwards he came to the United States, and happened to be the guest of a Clergyman. In the course of conversation concerning Rome and the Vatican, the matter was recalled to his recollection, and he mentioned that he had seen and read the Acta Pilati. It seems that the statement made a deep impression upon the mind of the latter, although it had been accompanied with the opinion that it did not add much to the common teachings of Christianity. Several months elapsed, but the statement of the learned German clung to the clergyman's memory. At last he could not forbear to write to him in New-York city, reminding him of the Acta Pilati, and asking whether it would not be possible to obtain a transcript of it from the Vatican. But he had already returned to his home in Westphalia. The letter was however forwarded; and finally, after much delay, an answer came, stating that he had written to Father Freelinhusen, a monk of great learning, at Rome, and custodian of the Vatican. He also stated that he had made the request in his own name, as he did not think the Papal authorities would be willing for such a document to go into the hands of the public. Father Freelinhusen expressed himself as willing to furnish the transcript. The parchment being old and defaced, he was compelled to use a magnifying glass in transcribing it. It was in the original Latin, and accompanied by the following letter:

"Rome, Italy, April 26th, 1859.

I hereby forward you the transcript as it is on record in the Vatican in Tiberius Cæsar's Court by Pilate. I certify this to be a true copy, word for word, as it occurs there.

PETER FREELINHUSEN."

For twenty years its owner has kept it as a private literary treasure. Not until now has he been induced by the importunate urgency of many esteemed friends to give it to the world.

As being the most ancient non-biblical testimony about Christ — antedating even the first of the Gospels and Epistles — it will be read with feelings of peculiar interest and even awe. Its publication will be welcomed by thousands who have seen references to it, and by all to whom this is the first notice of its existence. Without claiming that the Acta Pilati add materially to the sum of details furnished in the Gospels, they will nevertheless silence, forever, the cavils of all who have sneeringly asked, why profane historians have not mentioned the introduction of Christianity into the world. Indeed there is now accessible a complete chain of non-biblical testimony, each link comprising an important item in the life of our Savior. That Cæsar Augustus ordered the whole world to be taxed, we learn from Tacitus, Suetonius, and Dion; that a great Light or Star appeared in the East, from Chalcidius; the cruelty of Herod, even to the point of slaughtering innocent children and putting to death his own sons, is mentioned by Josephus; that our Savior had been in Egypt, by Celsus; that Pontius Pilate was Governor of Judea, by Tacitus; that miraculous cures, and works out of the ordinary course of nature were wrought by Christ, is distinctly stated by Julian the Apostate, Porphyry, and Hierocles; that Jesus made predictions which came to pass, and the earth-quake and darkness when he died, by Phlegon; and the immediate causes which led to the crucifixion, and the particulars of his trial, in the official report of Pilate himself.

THE ESTIMATION IN WHICH THE ACTA FILATI WERE HELD BY THE APOSTOLIC FATHERS AND EARLY DEFENDERS OF CHRISTIANITY.

The early Fathers of the Church deemed this document of the highest authority and value.

Justin Martyr, in his first apology for the Christians, which was presented to the Emperor Antoninus Pius, in the year A. D., 138, having mentioned the Crucifixion of Jesus and some of its attendant circumstances, says:

And that these things were so done, you may know from the Acts made in the time of Pontius Pilate."

Afterwards, in the same apology, having noticed some of our Lord's miracles, such as healing diseases and raising the dead, he says :

"And that these things were done by him, you may know by the Acts made in the time of Pontius Pilate." (Apol. Prima, 65, 72).

Justin Martyr was born A. D., 89. Joseph Addison says, concerning him, that "he resided, made converts, and suffered martyrdom at Rome, where he was engaged with Philosophers, and in a particular manner with one Crescens, the Cynic, who could easily have detected, and would not have failed to expose him, had he quoted a record not in being, or made any false citation out of it. Would the great Apologist have challenged Crescens to dispute the cause of Christianity with him, before the Roman Senate, had he forged such an evidence, or would Crescens have refused the challenge, could he have triumphed over him in the detection of such a forgery? To which we must add, that the apology which appeals to this record, was presented to a learned Emperor and to the whole body of the Roman Senate." (Addison's Evidence, edition London, 1776, p. 9).

The learned Tertullian, in his Apology for Christianity, about the year 200, after speaking of our Savior's crucifixion and resurrection, and his appearance to the disciples, who were ordained by him to publish the Gospel over the world, thus proceeds :

"Of all these things relating to Christ, Pilate himself, in his conscience already a Christian, sent an account to Tiberius, then Emperor."

The same writer, in the same Apology, thus relates the proceedings of Tiberius on receiving this information :

"There was an ancient decree that no one should be received for a deity unless he was first approved by the Senate. Tiberius, in whose time the Christian name [or religion] had its rise, having received from Palestine in Syria, an account of such things as manifested the truth of his [Christ's] divinity- proposed to the Senate that he should be enrolled among the Boman gods, and gave his own prerogative vote in favor of the motion. But the Senate [without whose consent no deification could take place] rejected it, because the Emperor himself had declined the same honor. Nevertheless. the Emperor persisted in his opinion. and threatened punishment to the accusers of the Christians. Search your own commentaries [or public writings], you will there find that Nero was the first who raged with the imperial sword against the sect, when rising most at Rome."

The value of the above citations is well expressed in the following language of the learned Horne, in his "Introduction to the Critical Study and Knowledge of the Holy Scriptures," vol. I, page 82. He says:

"These testimonies of Justin and Tertullian. are taken from public apologies for the Christian religion, which Avere presented either to the Emperor and Senate of Rome, or to magistrates of public authority and great distinction in the Roman empire. Now it is incredible that such writers would have made such appeals, especially to the very persons in whose custody these documents were, had they not been fully satisfied of their existence and contents."

The account which Eusebius gives of the Acta Pilati is very clear, and affords several particulars concerning the effect produced upon the mind of the Emperor Tiberius. He says :

"The fame of our Lord's remarkable resurrection and ascension being now spread abroad, according to an ancient custom prevalent among the rulers of the nations, to communicate novel occurrences to the Emperor, that nothing might escape him, Pontius Pilate transmits to Tiberius an account of the circumstances concerning the resurrection of our Lord from the dead, the report of which had already spread throughout all Palestine. In this account he also intimated that he ascertained other miracles respecting him, and that now having risen from the dead, he was believed to be a God by the great mass of the people. Tiberius referred the matter to the Senate, but it is said they rejected the proposition, apparently because they had not examined into this subject first, according to an ancient law among the Bomans, that no one should be ranked among the gods unless by a vote and decree of the Senate; in reality, however, because the salutary doctrine of the Gospel needs no confirmation and co-operation of men." * * * "Tiberius, therefore, under whom the name of Christ was spread throughout the world, when this doctrine was announced to him from Palestine, where it first began, communicated with the Senate, being obviously pleased with the doctrine; but the Senate, as they had not proposed the measure, rejected it. But he continued in his opinion, threatening death to the accusers of the Christians; a divine providence infusing this into his mind. that the Gospel having freer scope in its commencement, might spread everywhere over the world." (Eusebius Ecclesiastical History, Book H, chapter 2. page 74).

THE FORGERY OF THE ORIGINAL BY THE ENEMIES OF THE CHRISTIANS, A. D. 311.

The authority and force of the appeals to this document were felt and acknowledged by the Heathen opponents of Christianity to such a degree that during the reign of the Emperor Maximin, A. I). 311, false Acts of Pilate were forged, intended to cast discredit upon the Divine Founder of Christianity, and they were disseminated with the utmost activity. (See Milman's History of Christianity, page 266). Concerning the extent and bitterness to which this was carried, we also have the direct testimony of one who lived at the time. Eusebius says:

"Having forged, therefore, certain acts of Pilate, respecting our Saviour, full of every kind of blasphemy against Christ, these, with the consent of the Emperor, they sent through the whole of the Empire subject to him, commanding at the same time by ordinances in every place and city, and the adjacent districts, to publish these to all persons, and to give them to the schoolmasters to hand to their pupils to study and to commit to memory, as exercises for declamation. Whilst these things were doing, another commander. whom the Romans call Dux, in Damascus, a city of Phoenicia, caused certain infamous females to be seized from the forum, and threatening to inflict torture upon them, he forced them to make a formal declaration, taken down on record, that they had once been Christians, and that they were privy to the criminal acts among them : that in their very churches, they committed licentious deeds; and innumerable other slanders, which he wished them to utter against our religion; which declarations he inserted in the Acts, and communicated to the Emperor, who immediately commanded that these documents should be published in every city and place."

(Eusebius' Ecclesiastical History, Book IX, chapter 5, page 414).

THE VALUE OF THE ACTA FILATI.

The value of the Acta Pilati appears from the fact that it was deemed worthy of being travestied by the persecutors of the Christians ; from its dignified origin in the general usage of governments, ancient and modern, to re- quire important officers to render written reports of their administrations; that it was the means of preventing the Emperor Tiberius from persecuting the Christian church in its feeble infancy ; that it gave immense force to the arguments of the early Apologists that they could refer to the State Papers of the government for the truth of their statements; and besides all this, it is powerful collateral secular proof of the truth of the Gospel History.

1. Frolli the ancient testimonies already cited, it is at once evident *how important a place the Acta Pilati held in the estimation, of the Primitive Christians.* With what implicit and entire confidence Justin, Tertullian, and Eusebius rely upon it! It is prima facie evidence that it was often appealed to to be deemed worthy of being travestied when the enemies and persecutors of the Christians wanted weapons against them ! Had there been no such document, it could not have been counterfeited. Had it not been an important testimony, it would not have been forged. Both its actual existence and its apologetic importance are established by the falsification of it during the persecution under Maximin, A. D. 311.

2. It gives great dignity and force to the Acta Filati to bear in mind *that it originated, in the general usage of governments, ancient and modern, that important officers are to render written reports of their administrations.* In our own country the President sends his Message to Congress, together with the Annual Reports of the heads of the

various Departments. Similar to this was the custom in ancient times. In some such wav originated the Commentaries of Julius Cæsar, the letter of Agrippa to the Emperor Caligula, the famous Epistle of Pliny the younger to the Emperor Trajan, and many other documents still in existence. The Romans were particularly careful in preserving the memory of all remarkable events which occurred in their magnificent dominions. They had for this purpose, two sets of archives—the Acta Diurna Populi, and the Acta Senatus. Such reports were not published for general perusal, but deposited as State Papers of the Government, and served as a treasury of invaluable resources for the Annalist and the Historian.

Lord Beaconsfield tells us that" the Emperors were ambitious at length to give their names to the Libraries they founded; they did not consider the purple as their chief ornament. Augustus was himself an author, and in one of those sumptuous buildings called Thermes, ornamented with porticoes, galleries, and statues, with shady walks and refreshing baths, testified his love of literature by adding a magnificent library, one of those libraries he fondly called by the name of his sister, Octavia; and the other, the temple of Apollo, became the haunt of the poets, as Horace, Juvenal, and Persius have commemorated. The successors of Augustus imitated his example, *and even Tiberius had an Imperial library, chiefly consisting of works concerning the Empire, and the acts of its Sovereigns.* These Trajan augmented by the Ulpian library, so denominated from the family name of this prince." (Curiosities of Literature, page 1).

The fragments that remain in our day of these libraries and public documents constitute a part of the manuscript treasures of the Vatican at Rome; and there is a special alcove devoted to the records of Tiberius Cæsar, in which the original Latin text of the following English version is found. It is exceedingly difficult to gain access to these ancient and valuable manuscripts. They are guarded with the utmost care, and it is next to impossible to procure a copy of any of them, through any means. Even the English government, when a few years ago certain transcripts were wanted for the British Museum, were at first refused, and succeeded only after considerable negotiation. It is a singular and rare piece of good fortune that this copy of the Acta Pilati has been secured, in the manner already narrated.

3. The statement concerning *the impression it produced upon the mind of Tiberius* is of great interest and importance. We know from authentic sources that he was of a dark and brooding character, though possessed of great intellect. He was full of envy and suspicion, and easily aroused to acts of cruelty. His administration is darkened by many acts of injustice. It is very strange that he was not foremost among the persecutors of the Church. But instead of this we find a remarkable clemency and moderation towards the disciples of Jesus in his reign. It was then that the Christian Church had the opportunity to begin to grow. The Gospel was not nipped in the bud, but had free course and was spread abroad. In the profound impression produced by Pilate's writing, we have the link in the chain of Divine Providence that brought about this most desirable result.

4. One can easily imagine what power it gave to the early defenders of Christianity, *that they could appeal for the truth of their statements to the State papers of the Roman Empire.* They claimed that the official documents of the Civil Government confirmed the assertions they made in regard to Christ. A better argument could not be imagined. It makes the point It proves that these things which the Gospel narrates are not cunningly devised fables, and that they were not done in a corner; but that those best competent to do so were challenged at the time when they occurred to deny them, but were compelled to admit them as actual facts.

5.

6. It is a powerful argument for the truth of the Gospel, and from an entirely unique and independent stand-point. It is not from the pen of a Christian Apologist, but from the pen of a Heathen. It was written for a purely secular purpose; and yet it is, for all that, so much the more useful as a weapon in defense of Christianity. It is not an argument from a believer, stating the reasons of the hope that is in him, but merely an official report from an army officer to his superior, explaining why he had acted as he had done, under the peculiar circumstances which he explains. Its general burden and tone shows this to have been the only aim of the writer. It is indeed replete with weighty testimony to Jesus; but that is incidental and in no sense the main purpose of the writer. It is not an argument to prove the resurrection of Christ, or any other vital point; nor does he mention any important additional fact in which a believer in the Gospel would be likely to be interested. And yet it docs contain statements that do throw light upon the Gospel narrative, and that corroborate and explain it. *We may well, therefore, claim that we have here a powerful collateral secular proof of the truth of the Gospel History.*

7. We have before us, therefore, in the present volume, *the most ancient of all the secular testimonies to the New Testament.* The Roman historian, Suetonius, who flourished in the reign of the Emperor Trajan, A. D. 116, refers to Christ when he says that "Claudius Cæsar expelled the Jews from Rome, because they raised continual tumults at the instigation of Christ," who it is well known was sometimes called Chrestus, and his disciples Chrestians (Suetonius in Claudio, cap. 25). The event referred to occurred in the year A. D. 52, within twenty years after the Crucifixion. Tacitus, who flourished under Trajan, A. D. 110, writing the history of Nero, the successor of Claudius, A. D. 64, says of the Christians, "the author of that sect or name was Chrestus, who in the reign of Tiberius was punished with death as a criminal, by the Procurator Pontius Pilate," (Tacit. Annal. liber. XV, cap. 44).

Pliny the younger, in A. I). 107, says that Jesus was worshiped by his followers as God. (Plin. Epist. lib. X ep. 97, tom. II, p. 128).

The Acta Pilati antedates all these, and comes earlier even than the Syriac Letter of Mara, addressed to his son Serapeon A. I). 73. Mara, a man thoroughly versed in Greek Philosophy, but not satisfied with the consolations it offered, writes from his place of exile, a letter of comfort and instruction to his son, in which he ranks Christ along with Socrates and Pythagoras; he honors him as a wise king; he charges the Jews with his murder; declares that thereby they had brought upon themselves the destruction of their commonwealth, but that Christ continued to live in the new law which he had given. (Cureton, Spicil. Syria cum, London, 1855).

Weighty and important as these testimonies are, we yet claim for the Acta Pilati a still higher position. It has the advantage of priority; was probably composed in the very year of the Crucifixion, and is the utterance of an eye-witness to the momentous events it records. Pilate's report has all the more value to us, in that it is in no sense intended to be in the interest of Jesus, but that its original design was his own defence against possible accusation of maladministration.

8. This splendid document has thus been rescued from the corroding tooth of time, and from the accumulating dust of ages. It has doubtless, like the Holy Scriptures themselves, suffered many vicissitudes. As it is a curious circumstance in literary history that we should owe Tacitus to a single copy found in a monastery of Westphalia, so it is strange that the world should now receive the Acta Pilati from a single old and defaced copy in the Vatican. Thus the lapse of centuries, like the tides and storms of oceans, has doubtless swept into oblivion many great and stupendous events of history; but ever and anon borne up upon its bosom, from out the dark vast depths long hidden treasures, fresh as on the morning of their birth, and brilliant as the beams of the stars that shone on

nature's dawn.

> *"Truth is ever young, however old,*
>
> *'Tis ever new as when first told ;*
>
> *Its fragrance fresh as the new mould*
>
> *From which the first young flowers unfold."*

Truth shall outlive all the baneful plants of error. Out of hidden seeds of truth, dug from the hoary pyramids of time, that fling their shadows over the immeasurable wastes of sin's Sahara, shall grow flowery oases amid the fiery sands, — and blossom into good for man !

We print this book as the testimony of a Heathen, one who knew not the true God. *but one who saw and heard the Son of God !* It has been kept by the same hands, through which the Sacred Oracles themselves have been transmitted to us. It has now strangely come to light from under the care of keepers who have always jealously chained to the block of secrecy all they deemed too sacred for the masses of the people.

It comes at an opportune moment. The many Lives of Christ recently given to the world indicate the profound and unabated interest of mankind in Jesus. One of the greatest Theologians of the world says: "This is the religious question of the age;" and Goethe: "The conflict of faith and unbelief remains the proper, the only, the deepest theme of the history of the world and mankind, to which all others are subordinated." Even Renan says of Christ: "For thousands of years the world will depend on thee! Banner of our contests, thou shalt be the standard about which the hottest battle will be given. A thousand times more alive, a thousand times more beloved since thy

31

death than during thy passage here below, thou shalt become the corner-stone of humanity so entirely, that. to tear thy name from this world would be to rend it to its foundations." And William Cullen Bryant, in the same strain, but with still greater beauty of expression and depth of feeling:

"This character, of which Christ was the perfect model, is in itself so attractive, so 'altogether lovely,' that I cannot describe in language the admiration with which I regard it; nor can I express the gratitude I feel for the dispensation which bestowed that example on mankind, for the truths which he taught and the sufferings he endured for our sakes. I tremble to think what the world would be without Him. Take away the blessings of the advent of his life and the blessings purchased by his death, in what an abyss of guilt would man have been left ! It would seem to be blotting the sun out of the heavens — to leave our system of worlds in chaos, frost, and darkness.

"In my view of the life, the teachings, the labors, and the sufferings of the blessed Jesus, there can be no admiration too profound, no love of which the human heart is capable, too warm, no gratitude too earnest and deep of which he is justly the object. It is with sorrow that my love for him is so cold, and my gratitude so inadequate. It is with sorrow that I see any attempt to put aside His teachings as a delusion, to turn men's eyes from his example, to meet with doubt and denial the story of his life. For my part, if I thought the religion of skepticism were to gather strength and prevail and become the dominant view of mankind, I should despair of the fate of mankind in the years that are yet to come." (Alden, Thoughts on the Religious Life, with Introduction by W. Cullen Bryant. N. Y. Putnam, 1879).

In the elucidation of this question of questions, the most important phase is the historical aspect. The actual fact of the Life and Death of Jesus is just as capable of historic evidence as any other event of history.

In this direction the present volume is destined to accomplish a great mission. Unbelievers demand heathen testimony concerning the contents of the books of the New Testament. Here it is in abundance. The Kings and Congresses and Governments of Nations shall know — despite all that skeptical scientists, philosophers, and critics have done or can do, — that in the splendor of the Augustan age there came One, whose name shall outshine all the pomp and glory of worldly power and triumph; — and to whom all the nations of the world, not in mockery but in worship shall bend the knee; — and crown with a diadem not of thorns, but of praise and gratitude — the Lord of Lords and King of Kings.

ACTA PILATI.

The references indicated by the small letters throughout the text of the Acta, point to the NOTES, in which will be found all the principal historical and critical information necessary to its appreciative and enjoyable perusal.

Pontius PILATE[a] to the Emperor Tiberius;[b] Greeting: Recent events in my province have been of such a character, that I thought I would give the details as they have occurred, as I should not be surprised it in the course of time they may change the destiny of our nation, for it seems of late that the gods have ceased to be propitious. I am almost ready to say: Cursed be the day that I succeeded Valerius Gratus in the government of Judea. On my arrival at Jerusalem I took possession of the Pretorium and ordered a splendid feast to be prepared, to which I invited the tetrarch of Galilee, with the high Priests and his officers. At the appointed hour no guests appeared. This was an insult offered to my dignity. A few days after, the high priest deigned to pay me a visit. His deportment was grave and deceitful. He pretended that his religion forbade him and his attendants to sit down at the table of the Romans and to offer up libations with them. I thought it expedient to accept his excuse, but from that moment I was convinced that the conquered had declared themselves the enemies of the conquerors. It seemed to me of all conquered cities, Jerusalem was the most difficult to govern. So turbulent were the people that I lived in momentary dread of an insurrection. To suppress it I had but a single centurian and a handful of soldiers. I requested a reinforcement from the Prefect of Syria, who informed me that he had scarcely troops sufficient to defend his own province. An insatiate thirst for conquest — to extend our empire beyond the means of defending it — I fear will be the means of destroying our noble government.

Among the various rumors that came to my ears, there was one that attracted my attention in particular. A young man, it was said, had appeared in Galilee, preaching with a noble unction a new law, in the name of the gods that had sent him. At first I was apprehensive that his design was to stir up the people against the Romans, but soon were my fears dispelled. Jesus of Nazareth spake rather as a friend of the Romans than of the Jews.

One day in passing by the place of Siloe, where there was a great concourse of people, I observed in the midst of the group, a young man who was leaning against a tree, calmly addressing the multitude. I was told it was Jesus. This I could easily have suspected, so great was the difference between him and those who were listening to him. His golden colored hair and beard gave to his appearance a celestial aspect. He appeared to be about thirty years of age. Never have I seen a Sweeter or more serene countenance. What a contrast between him and his hearers, with their black beards and tawny complexion. Unwilling to interrupt him by my presence. I continued my walk; but signified to my secretary to join the group and listen. My secretary's name was Manlius. He was the grandson of the chief of the conspirators who encamped in Etruria Availing Cataline. Manlius was an ancient inhabitant of Judea, and well acquainted with the Hebrew language. He was devoted to me, and worthy of my confidence. On entering the Pretorium I found Manlius, who related to me the words Jesus had pronounced at Siloe. Never have I heard in the Pettico, nor in the works of the philosophers anything that can compare to the maxims of Jesus.

One of the rebellious Jews so numerous in Jerusalem, having asked him if it was lawful to give tribute to Cæsar, Jesus replied: "Render unto Cæsar the things which belong to Cæsar, and unto God the things that are God's." It was on account of the wisdom of this saying, that I granted so much liberty to the Nazarene, for it was in my power to have him arrested and exiled to Pontus; but this would have been contrary to the justice which has always characterized the Romans. This man was neither seditious nor rebellious. I extended to him my protection, unknown perhaps to himself. He was at liberty to act, to speak, to assemble and address the people, to choose disciples unrestrained by any Pretorian mandate. Should it ever happen — may the gods ever avert the omen — should it ever happen, I say, that the religion of our forefathers be supplanted by the religion of Jesus, it will be to this noble toleration that Rome shall owe her premature obsequies; while I, miserable wretch, shall have been the instrument of what the Hebrews call providence, and we, destiny.

But this unlimited freedom granted to Jesus provoked the Jews; not the poor, but the rich and powerful. It is true that Jesus was severe on the latter; and this was a political reason, in my opinion, not to control the liberty of the Nazarene. "Scribes and Pharisees," he would say to them, "you arc a race of vipers; you resemble painted sepulchres." At other times he would sneer at the proud alms of the publican, telling him that the mite of the poor widow was more precious in the sight of God.

New complaints were daily made at the Pretorium against the insolence of Jesus. I was even informed that some misfortune would befall him — that it would not be the first time that Jerusalem had stoned those who called themselves prophets — and if the Pretorinm refused justice an appeal[c] would be made to Cæsar. However, my conduct was approved by the Senate, and I was promised a reinforcement after the termination of the Parthian war. Being too weak to suppress a sedition, I resolved upon adopting a measure that promised to establish the tranquility of the city, without subjecting the Pretorium to humilating concession.

I wrote to Jesus, requesting an interview with him at the Pretorium. You know that in my veins flows the Spanish, mixed with the Roman blood, as incapable of fear as it is of puerile emotion. When the Nazarene made his appearance I was walking in my basilic, and my feet seemed fastened with an iron hand to the marble pavement, and I trembled in every limb as a guilty culprit, though he was calm — the Nazarene, calm as innocence. When he came up to me he stopped, and by a signal sign he seemed to say to me, "I am here." For some time, I contemplated with admiration and awe this extraordinary type of man — a type of man unknown to our numerous painters, who have given form and figure to all the gods and heroes.

"Jesus," I said to him at last — and my tongue faltered — " Jesus of Nazareth, I have granted you for the last three years ample freedom of speech, nor do I regret it. Your words are those of a sage. I know not whether you have read Socrates or Plato, but this I know, that there is in your discourses a majestic simplicity that elevates you far above these philosophers. The Emperor is informed of it, and I, his humble representative in this country, am glad of having allowed you that liberty of which you are so worthy. However, I must not conceal from you that your discourses have raised up against you powerful and inveterate enemies. Neither is this surprising. Socrates had his enemies, and he fell a victim of their hatred. Yours are doubly incensed against you, on account of your sayings against them, and on account of the liberty extended towards you. They even accused me of being indirectly leagued with you, for the purpose of depriving the Hebrews of the little civil power which Rome has left them.[d] My request — I do not say my order — is, that you be more circumspect in the future, and more tender in arousing the pride of your enemies, lest they raise against you the stupid populace, and compel me to employ the instruments of justice.

The Nazarene calmly replied: "Prince of the earth, your words proceed not from true wisdom.[e] Say to the torrent, stop in the midst of the mountain home, because it will uproot the trees of the valley. The torrent will answer you, that it must obey the laws of the Creator. God alone knows whither flows the torrent. Verily, I say unto you, before the Rose of Sharon blossoms, the blood of the just shall be spilt."

"Your blood shall not be spilt," replied I with emotion. " You are more precious, in my estimation, on account of your wisdom, than all the turbulent and proud Pharisees, who abuse the freedom granted them by the Romans, conspire against Cæsar, and construe our bounty into fear. Insolent wretches, they are not aware that the wolf of the Tiber sometimes clothes himself with the skin of the sheep. I will protect you against them. My Pretorium is open to you as an asylum; it is a sacred asylum."

Jesus carelessly shook his head, and said, with a grace and a divine smile, "When the day shall have come, there will be no asylum for the Son of Man, neither in the earth nor under the earth. The asylum of the Just is there, pointing to the heavens. That which is written in the books of the prophets must be accomplished.

"Young man," answered I, mildly, "you oblige me to convert my request into an order. The safety of the province, which has been confided to my care, requires it. You must observe more moderation in your discourses. Do not infringe. My orders you know. May happiness attend you. Farewell."

"Prince of the earth," replied Jesus, "I come not to bring war into the world, but peace, love and charity. I was born on the same day on which Augustus Cæsar gave peace to the Roman world. Persecution proceeds not from me. I expect it from others, and will meet it in obedience to the will of my Father, who has shown me the way. Restrain therefore, your worldly prudence. It is not in your power to arrest the victim at the foot of the Tabernacle of expiation."

So saying, he disappeared like a bright shadow behind the curtains of the basilic. To Herod, who then reigned in Galilee, the enemies of Jesus addressed themselves, to wreak their vengeance on the Nazarene. Had Herod consulted his own inclination, he would have ordered Jesus immediately to be put to death; but, though proud of his royal dignity, yet he was afraid of committing an act that might diminish his influence with the Senate. Herod called on me one day at the Pretorium, and on rising to take leave, after some insignificant conversation, he asked me what was my opinion concerning the Nazarene. I replied that Jesus appeared to be one of those great philosophers that great nations sometimes produce, that his doctrines are by no means sacrilegious, and that the intention of Rome was to leave him to that freedom of speech which was justified by his actions. Herod smiled maliciously, and saluting me with an ironical respect, he departed.

The great feast of the Jews was approaching, and the intention was to avail themselves of the popular exultation which always manifests itself at the solemnities of a pass- over. The city was overflowing with a tumultuous populace clamoring for the death of the Nazarene. My emissaries informed me that the treasure of the Temple had been employed in bribing the people. The danger was pressing. A Roman centurion had been insulted. I wrote to the prefect of Syria for a hundred foot soldiers, and as many cavalry. He declined. I saw myself alone, with a handful of veterans, in the midst of a rebellious city, too weak to suppress a disorder, and having no other choice left but to tolerate it. They had seized upon Jesus; and the seditious rabble, although they had nothing to fear from the Pretorium, believing with their leaders that I winked at their sedition, continued vociferating, "Crucify him! crucify him!" Three powerful parties had combined together at that time against Jesus. First, the Herodians and the Sadducees, whose seditious conduct seemed to have proceeded from double motives. They hated the Nazarene, and were impatient of the Roman yoke. They could never forgive me for having entered the holy city with banners that bore the image of the Roman Emperor, and, although in this instance I had committed a fatal error, yet the sacrilege did not appear less heinous in their eyes. Another grievance, also, rankled in their bosoms. I had proposed to employ a part of the treasure of the Temple in erecting edifices of public utility. My proposal was scowled at. The

Pharisees were the avowed enemies of Jesus. They cared not for the government. They bore with bitterness the severe reprimands which the Nazarene for three years had been continually throwing out against them wherever he went. Too weak and pusillanimous to act by themselves, they had embraced the quarrels of the Herodians and the Sadducees. Besides these three parties, I had to contend against the reckless and profligate populace, always ready to join a sedition, and to profit by the disorder and confusion that resulted therefrom.

Jesus was dragged before the high priest and condemned to death. It was then that the high priest, Caiaphas, performed a derisory act of submission. He sent his prisoner to me to pronounce his condemnation, and secure his execution.[f] I answered him, that as Jesus was a Galilean, the affair came in Herod's jurisdiction, and ordered him to be sent hither. The wily tetrarch professed humility, and protesting his preference to the Lieutenant of Cæsar, he committed the fate of the man to my hands. Soon my palace assumed the aspect of a besieged citadel. Every moment increased the number of the seditionists. Jerusalem was inundated with crowds from the mountains of Nazareth. All Judea appeared to be pouring into the devoted city. I had taken a wife[g] — a girl from among the Gauls — who professed to see into futurity — weeping and throwing herself at my feet — " Beware," said she to me, "beware, and touch not that man, for he is holy. Last night I saw him in a vision. He was walking on the waters. He was flying on the wings of the winds. He spoke to the tempest, and to the fishes of the lake — all were obedient to him. Behold ! the torrent in Mount Kedron flows with blood, the statues of Cæsar are filled with Gemoniae,[h] the columns of the Interinili have given away, and the sun is veiled in mourning, like a vestal in the tomb. O Pilate! evil awaits thee if thou wilt not listen to the vows of thy wife. Dread the curse of a Roman Senate, dread the powers of Cæsar."

By this time the marble stairs groaned under the weight of the multitude. The Nazarene was brought back to me. I proceeded to the hall of justice, followed by my guard, and asked the people, in a severe tone, what they demanded. "The death of the Nazarene," was the reply. "For what crime?" "He has blasphemed. He has prophesied the ruin of the Temple. He calls himself the Son of God, the Messiah, the King of the Jews." "Roman justice," said I, "punishes not such offenses with death." "Crucify him, crucify him!" belched forth the relentless rabble. The vociferations of the infuriated mob shook the palace to its foundations. There was but one who appeared to be calm in the midst of the vast multitude. It was the Nazarene. After many fruitless attempts to protect him from this fury of his merciless persecutors, I adopted a measure which, at the moment, appeared to me to be the only one that could save his life. I ordered him to be scourged, then calling for an ewer, I washed my hands[i] in the presence of the multitude, thereby signifying to them my disapproval of the deed. But in vain. It was his life that these wretches thirsted for. Often in our civil commotions have I witnessed the furious animosity of the multitude, but nothing could be compared to what I witnessed in the present instance. It might have been truly said, that on this occasion all the phantoms of the infernal regions had assembled at Jerusalem.

The crowd appeared not to walk; they were borne off, and whirled as a vortex, rolling along like living waves, from the portals of the Pretorium even unto Mount Zion, with bowlings, screams, shrieks, and vociferations, such as were never heard in the seditions of the Panonia, or in the tumult of the forum.

By degrees the day darkened like a winter's twilight, such as had been at the death of the great Julius Cæsar. It was likewise towards the ides of March.

I, the continued governor of a rebellious province, was leaning against a column of my basilic, contemplating athwart the dreary gloom of these fiends of tartars dragging to execution the innocent Nazarene. All around me was deserted. Jerusalem had vomited forth her indwellers through the funeral gate that leads to the Gemonica. An air of desolation and sadness enveloped me. My guards had joined the cavalry, and the centurion, to display a shadow of power, was endeavoring to keep order. I was left alone, and my breaking heart admonished me that what was passing at that moment appertained rather to the history of the gods than that of man. A loud clamor was heard proceeding from Golgotha, which, borne on the winds, seemed to announce an agony such as had never been heard by mortal ears. Dark clouds lowered over the pinnacle of the temple, and, settling over the city, covered it with a veil. So dreadful were the signs that were seen, both in the heavens and on the earth, that Dionysius, the Areopagite,[k] is reported to have exclaimed, " Either the author of nature is suffering, or the universe is falling apart."

Towards the first hour of the night,[l] I threw my mantle around me and went down into the city, toward the gates of Golgotha. The sacrifice was consummated. The crowd was returning home; still agitated, it is true; but gloomy, taciturn and desperate. What they had witnessed had stricken them with terror and remorse. I also saw my little Roman cohort pass by mournfully, the standard- bearer having veiled his eagle in token of grief, and I overheard some of the soldiers murmuring strange words, which I did not understand. Others were recounting prodigies almost similar to those which had so often smitten the Romans by the will of the gods. Sometimes groups of men and women would halt, then looking backward towards Golgotha, would remain motionless, in expectation of witnessing some new prodigy.

I returned to the Pretorium, sad and pensive. On ascending the stairs — the steps of which were still stained with the blood of the Nazarene—I perceived an old man in a suppliant posture, and behind him several women in tears. He threw himself at my feet and wept bitterly. It is painful to see an old man weep.

"Father," said I to him mildly, "who are you and what is your request?"

"I am Joseph of Arimathea," replied he, "and am come to beg of you, upon my knees, the permission to bury Jesus of Nazareth."

"Your prayer is granted," said I to him, and at the same time ordered Manlius to take some soldiers with him to superintend the interment, Jest it should be profaned.

A few days after, the sepulchre was found empty. His disciples published all over the country that Jesus had risen from the dead, as he had foretold. A last duty remained for me to perform, and that was to communicate to you these deplorable events. I did it on the same night that followed the fatal catastrophe, and had just finished the communication when day began to dawn. At that moment the sound of clarions playing the air of Diana, struck my ear. Casting my eye towards the Cæsarean gate I beheld a troop of soldiers, and heard at a distance other trumpets sounding Cæsar's march. It was the reinforcement that had been promised me. Two thousand chosen troops who, to hasten their arrival, had marched all night. " It has been decreed by the fates," cried I, wringing my hands, " that the great iniquity should be accomplished; that for the purpose of averting the deeds of yesterday, troops should arrive to-day ! Cruel destiny, how thou sportesi with the affairs of mortals!" It was but too true, what the Nazarene exclaimed while writhing on the cross : " All is consummated."

HISTORICAL
AND
CRITICAL NOTES.

A BRIEF SKETCH OF THE LIFE OF

PONTIUS PILATE.

Pontius Pilate was the sixth Roman Procurator of Judea, (Matt. xxvii: 2; Mark xv: 1; Luke iii: 1; John xviii-xix), under whom our Lord taught, suffered and died (Acts iii: 13; iv:27; xiii: 28; I Tim. vi: 13; Tacit. Annal. xv:44). The testimony of Tacitus on this point is no less clear than it is important; for it fixes beyond a doubt the time when the foundations of our religion were laid. The words of the great historian are: *"Auctor nominis ejus Christus. Tiberio imperitante per Procuratorem Pontium Pilatura supplicio affectus est.* – 'The author of that name (Christian) or sect was Christ, who was capitally punished in the reign of Tiberius by Pontius Pilate."

Pilate was the successor of Valerius Gratus, and governed Judea, in the reign of Tiberius. He held his office for a period of ten years. The agreement on this point between the accounts in the New Testament and those supplied by Josephus, is entire and satisfactory. It has been exhibited in detail by the learned, accurate and candid Lardner (Vol. I, 150-389, Lond. 1827).

Pilate's conduct in his office was, in many respects, highly culpable. Josephus has recorded two instances in which Pilate acted very tyrannically (Antiq. xviii:3, I; comp. De Bell. Jud. ii: 9, 2, sq.) in regard to the Jews. "But now Pilate, the Procurator of Judea, removed the army from Cæsarea to Jerusalem, to take their winter-quarters there, in order to abolish the Jewish laws. So he introduced Cæsar's effigies, which were upon the ensigns, and brought them into the city; whereas our law forbids us the very making of images;

on which account the former procurators were wont to make their entry into the city with such ensigns as had not those ornaments. Pilate was the first who brought those images to Jerusalem, and set them up there: which was done without the knowledge of the people, because it was done in the night-time; but, as soon as they knew it, they came in multitudes to Cæsarea, and interceded with Pilate many days, that he would remove the images; and when he would not grant their request, because this would tend to the injury of Cæsar, while they yet persevered in their request, on the sixth day he ordered his soldiers to have their weapons privately, while he came and sat upon his judgement-seat; which seat was so prepared in the open place of the city, that it concealed the army that lay ready to oppress them : and when the Jews petitioned him again, he gave a signal to the soldiers to encompass them round, and threatened that their punishment should be no less than immediate death, unless they would leave off disturbing him, and go their ways home. But they threw themselves on the ground, and laid their necks bare, and said they would take their death very willingly, rather than the wisdom of their laws should be transgressed; upon which Pilate was deeply affected with their resolution to keep their laws inviolable, and presently ordered the images to be carried back from Jerusalem to Cæsarea."

"But Pilate undertook to bring a current of water to Jerusalem, and did it with the sacred money, and derived the origin of the stream from a distance of 200 furlongs. However the Jews were not pleased with what had been done about this water; and many ten thousands of the people got together and made a clamor against him, and insisted that he should leave off that design. Some of them also used reproaches, and abused the man, as crowds of such people usually do. So he habited a great number of his soldiers in their habit, who carried daggers under their garments, and sent them to a place where they might surround them. He bid the Jews himself go away; but they boldly casting reproaches upon him, he gave the soldiers the signal which had been before agreed on, who laid upon them much greater blows than Pilate had commanded them, and equally punished those that were tumultuous and those that were not; nor did they spare them in the least; and since the people were unarmed, and were caught by men prepared for what they were about, there were a great number of them slain by this means, and others of them ran away wounded. And thus an end was put to this sedition."

"We have," says Lardner, "another attempt of Pilate's of the same nature, mentioned in the letter which Agrippa the Elder sent to Caligula, as this letter is given us by Philo. In some particulars it has a great resemblance with the story Josephus has told of Pilate's bringing the ensigns into Jerusalem, and in others it is very different from it; which has given occasion to some learned men to suppose that Philo has been mistaken. For my own part, as I make no doubt but Josephus' account of the ensigns is true, so I think that Philo may also be relied on for the truth of a fact he has mentioned, as happening in his own time in Judea, and consequently, I judge them to be two different facts."

Agrippa, reckoning up to Caligula the several favors conferred on the Jews by the Imperial family, says: "Pilate was procurator of Judea. He, not so much out of respect to Tiberius as a malicious intent to vex the people, dedicates gilt shields, and places them in Herod's palace within the holy city. There was no figure upon them, nor anything else which is forbidden, except an inscription which expressed these two things — the name of the person who dedicated them, and of him to whom they were dedicated. When the people perceived what had been done, they desired that this innovation of the shields might be rectified; that their ancient customs which had been preserved through so many ages, and had hitherto been untouched by kings and emperors, might not now be violated. He refused their demands with roughness, such was his temper, fierce and untractable. They then cried out, Do not you raise a sedition yourself; do not you disturb the peace by your illegal practices. It is not Tiberius' pleasure that any of our laws should be broken in upon. If you have received any edict or letter from the emperor to this purpose, produce it, that we may leave you, and depute an embassy to him, and entreat him to revoke his orders. This put him out of all temper; for he was afraid if they should send an embassy, they might discover the many maladministrations of his government; his extortions, his unjust decrees, his inhuman cruelties. This reduced him to the utmost perplexity. On the one hand he was afraid to remove things that had been once dedicated, and was also unwilling to do a favor to men that were his subjects; and, on the other hand, he knew very well the inflexible severity of Tiberius. The chief men of the nation observing this, and perceiving that he repented of what he had done, though he endeavored to conceal it, wrote a most humble and submissive letter to Tiberius. It is needless to say how he was provoked when he read the account of Pilate's speeches and threatenings, the event showing it sufficiently. For he soon sent a letter to Pilate, reprimanding him for so audacious a proceeding; requiring, also, that the shields be removed. And, accordingly they were carried from the metropolis to Cæsarea by the seaside, called Sebaste, from your great grandfather, that they might be placed in the temple there consecrated to him, and there they were re- posited."

To the Samaritans, also, Pilate conducted himself unjustly and cruelly. His own misconduct led the Samaritans to take a step which in itself does not appear seditious or revolutionary, when Pilate seized the opportunity to slay many of the people, not only in the fight which ensued, but also in cold blood after they had given themselves up.

"But when this tumult was appeased, the Samaritan Senate sent an embassy to Vitellins, now President of Syria, and accused Pilate of the murder of those who had been slain. So Vitellins sent Marcellus, a friend of his, to take care of the affairs of Judea, and ordered Pilate to go to Rome to answer before the Emperor to the accusations of the Jews. Pilate, when he had tarried ten years in Judea, made haste to Rome, and this in obedience to the orders of Vitellus, which he durst not contradict; but before he could get to Rome, Tiberius was dead." (Joseph. Antiq. xviii. 4. 2.) This removal took place before the passover, in A. D. 36 — probably about September or October, A. D. 35; Pilate must, therefore, as he spent ten years in Judea, have entered on his government about October, A. D. 25, or at least before the Passover, A. D. 26, in the twelfth year of Tiberius' sole empire. (Compare Lardner I, 391, sq.; Winer, Real-worterb.).

To be put out of his government by Vitellus, on the complaint of the people of his province, must have been a very grevions mortification to Pilate; and though the emperor was dead before he reached Rome, he did not long enjoy such impunity as guilt permits; he was banished to Vienna in Gaul, and as Eusebius (Chron. p. 78) states, he shortly afterwards made way with himself, out of vexation for his many misfortunes, about A. D. 38.

Owing to the atrocity of the deed in which Pilate took a principal part, a very unfavorable view has generally been entertained of his character. Still it is interesting to note that the early Christians entertained a deep appreciation of his efforts to save Jesus. Tertullian, as already quoted on page 21, uses the expression, " Pilate himself in his conscience already a Christian." The Evang. Nicod. I:13. speaks of him as " circumsized in heart." According to one tradition he died a Christian Martyr, and to this day the Abyssinian Church celebrates the event on June 25.

There is great weight in the following language of a great critic:

"If now we wish to form a judgement of Pilate's character, we easily see that he was one of that large class of men who aspire to public offices, not from a pure and lofty desire of benefiting the public and advancing the good of the world, but from selfish and personal considerations, from a love of distinction, from a love of power, from a love of self-indulgence; being destitute of any fixed principles, and having no aim but office and influence, they act right only by chance and when convenient, and are wholly incapable of pursuing a consistent course, or of acting with firmness and self-denial in cases in which the preservation of integrity requires the exercise of these qualities. Pilate was obviously a man of weak, and therefore, with his temptations, of corrupt character. The view given in the Apostolical Constitutions (v. 14), where unmanliness is ascribed to him, we take to be correct. This Avant of strength will readily account for his failure to rescue Jesus from the rage of his enemies, and also for the acts of injustice and cruelty which he practiced in his government — acts which, considered in themselves, wear a deeper dye than does the conduct which he observed in surrendering Jesus to the malice of the Jews. And this same weakness may serve to explain to the reader bow much influence would be exerted on this unjust judge, not only by the stern bigotry, and persecuting wrath of the Jewish priesthood, but specially by the not concealed intimations which they threw out against Pilate, that, if he liberated Jesus, he was no friend of Tiberius, and must expect to have to give an account of his conduct at Rome. And that this was no idle threat, nothing beyond the limits of probability, Pilate's subsequent deposition by Vitellius shows very plainly; nor could the procurator have been ignorant either of the stern determination of the Jewish character, or of the offence he had by his acts given to the heads of the nation, or of the insecurity, at that very hour, when the contest between him and the priests was proceeding regarding the innocent victim whom they lusted to destroy, of his own position in the office which he held, and which, of course, he desired to retain. On the whole, then, viewing the entire conduct of Pilate, his previous iniquities as well as his bearing on the condemnation of Jesus — viewing his own actual position and the malignity of the Jews, we cannot, we confess, give our vote with those who have passed the severest condemnation on this weak and guilty governor." (See Kitto's Cyclopædia of Biblical Literature; Winer's Real Woerterbuch, and Farrar's Life of Christ.)

(Note b, page 47.)

A BRIEF SKETCH OF THE LIFE OF

THE EMPEROR TIBERIUS.

Claudius Drusus Nero Tiberius, the Roman emperor after the death of Augustus, was decended from the family of the Claudii. In his early years he commanded popularity by entertaining the populace with magnificent shows and fights of gladiators, and he gained some applause in the funeral oration which he pronounced over his father, though only nine years old. His first appearance in the Roman armies was under Augustus, in the war against the Cantabri, and afterwards, in the capacity of General, he gained victories in different parts of the Empire, and was rewarded with a triumph.

Yet in the midst of his glory, Tiberius fell under the displeasure of Augustus, and retired to Rhodes, where he continued for seven years as an exile, till by the influence of his mother, Livia, with the emperor, he was recalled. His return to Rome was the more glorious; he had the command of the Roman armies in Illyricum, Pannonia, and Dalmatia, and seemed to divide the sovereign power with Augustus.

At the death of this celebrated emperor, Tiberius, who had been adopted, assumed the reins of government; and while with dissimulation and affected modesty he wished to decline the dangerous office, he found time to try the fidelity of his friends, and to make the greatest part of the Romans believe that he was invested with the purple, not from his own choice, but by the recommendation of Augustus and the urgent entreaties of the Roman Senate. The beginning of his reign seemed to promise tranquillity to the world. Tiberius was a watchful guardian of the public peace, he was a friend of justice. and never assumed the sounding title which must disgust a free nation; but he was satis- tied to say of himself, that he was the master of his slaves, the general of his soldiers, and the father of the citizens of Rome. That seeming moderation however, which was but the fruit of the deepest policy, soon disappeared, and Tiberius was viewed in his real character. His ingratitude to his mother Livia, to whose intrigues he was indebted for the purple, his cruelty to his wife Julia, and his tyrannical oppression and murder of many noble senators, rendered him odious to the people, and suspected even by his most intimate favorites.

The armies mutinied in Pannonia and Germany, but the tumults were silenced by the prudence of the generals and the fidelity of the officers, and the factious demagogues were abandoned to punishment. This acted as a check on Tiberius at Rome; he knew from thence, as his successors experienced, that his power was precarious, and his very existence in perpetual danger. He continued, as he had begun, to pay the greatest deference to the Senate; all libels against him he disregarded, and observed, that in a free city the thoughts and the tongue of every man should be free. The taxes were gradually lessened and luxury restrained by the salutary regulations, as well as by the prevailing- example and frugality of the Emperor. While Rome exhibited a scene of peace and public tranquillity, the barbarians were severally defeated on the borders of the empire, and Tiberius gained new honors by the activity and valour of Germanicus and his other faithful lieutenants. Yet the triumphs of Germanicus Avere beheld with jealousy.

Tiberius dreaded his power; he was envious of his popularity; and the death of that celebrated general in Antioch was, as some suppose, accelerated by poison and the secret resentment of the emperor. Not only his relations and friends, but the great and opulent were sacrificed to his ambition, cruelty and avarice; and there was scarce in Rome one single family that did not reproach Tiberius for the loss of a brother, a father or a husband. He at last retired to the island of Capreae, on the coast of Campania, where he buried himself in unlawful pleasures. The care of the empire was entrusted to favorites, among whom Sejanus shone for awhile with uncommon splendor. In his solitary retreat the emperor proposed rewards to such as invented new pleasures, or could procure fresh luxuries. He forgot his age as well as his dignity, and disgraced himself by the most unnatural vices and enormous indulgences which can draw a blush, even on the countenance of the most debauched and abandoned.

While the emperor was lost to himself and the world, the provinces were harassed on every side by the barbarians, and Tiberius found himself insulted by those enemies whom hitherto he had seen fall prostrate at his feet with every mark of submissive adulation. At last, grown weak and helpless through infirmities, he thought of his approaching dissolution; and as he well knew that Rome could not exist without a head, he nominated as his successor Caius Caligula. Many might enquire why a youth naturally so vicious and abandoned as Caius was chosen to be the master of an extensive empire: but Tiberius wished his own cruelties to be forgotten in the barbarities which might be displayed in the reign of his successor, whose natural propensities he had well defined, in saying of Caligula, that he bred a serpent for the Roman people, and a Phaeton for the rest of the empire. Tiberius died at Misenum the 16th of March, A. D. 37, in the 78th year of his age, after a reign of 22 years, 6 months and 26 days. Caligula was accused of having hastened his end by suffocating him.

The joy was universal when his death was known ; and the people of Rome, in the midst of sorrow, had a moment to rejoice, heedless of the calamities which awaited them in the succeeding reigns. The body of Tiberius was conveyed to Rome and burnt with great solemnity. A funeral oration was pronounced by Caligula, who seemed to forget his benefactor while he expatiated on the praises of Augustus, Germanicus and his own. The character of Tiberius has been examined with particular attention by historians, and his reign is the subject of the most perfect and elegant of all the compositions of Tacitus. When a private man, Tiberius was universally esteemed; when he had no superior he was proud, arrogant, jealous and revengeful. If he found his military operations conducted by a warlike general, he affected moderation and virtue; but when he got rid of the powerful influence of a favorite, he was tyrannical and dissolute. If, as some observed, he had lived in the times of the Roman republic, be might have been as conspicuous as his great ancestors; but the sovereign power lodged in his hands rendered him vicious and oppressive.

Yet, though he encouraged informers and favored flattery, he blushed at the mean survilities of the Senate, and derided the adulation of his courtiers, who approached him, he said, as if they approached a savage elephant. He was a patron of learning, he was an eloquent and ready speaker, and dedicated some part of his time to study. He wrote a lyric poem, entitled, "A complaint on the death of Lucius Cæsar;" as also some Greek pieces in imitation of some of his favorite authors. He avoided all improper expressions, and all foreign words he wished to totally banish from the Latin tongue. As instances of his humanity, it has been recorded that he was uncommonly liberal to the people of Asia Minor, whose habitations had been destroyed by a violent earthquake, A. D. 17. One of his officers wished him to increase the taxes. No, said Tiberius, a good shepherd must shear, but not flay his sheep. The Senators wished to call the month of November, in which he was born, by his name, in imitation of J. Cæsar and Augustus, in the months of July and August; but this he refused, saying : "What will you do, conscript fathers, if you have thirteen Cæsars?" Like the rest of the emperors, he received divine honors after death, and even during life. (From Bibliotheca Classica, by Lempriere. See also Niehbuhr's History of Rome, Vol. IV. Lecture LXI, and especially Stahr, Tiberius, Leben, Regierung, Charakter, 2d ed. 1873).

(Note c, page 53.;

APPEAL TO CÆSAR.

From the whole tone of the Acta, — and it is fully corroborated by contemporaneous history, — Pilate was anxious to avoid an appeal to Cæsar. " That Cæsar was the dark and jealous Tiberius. Up to this period the Jewish nation, when they had complained of the tyranny of their native sovereigns, had ever obtained a favorable hearing at Pome. Even against Herod the Great their charges had been received; they had been admitted to a public audience; and though their claim to national independence at the death of that sovereign had not been allowed, Archelaus had received his government with limited powers, and, on the complaint of the people, had been removed from his throne. In short, the influence of that attachment to the Cæsarean family, which had obtained for the nation distinguished privileges both from Julius and Augustus, had not yet been effaced by that character of turbulence and insubordination which led to their final ruin." (Milman's Hist. of Christianity, page 140).

(Note d, page 55.)

THE RELATIONS OF THE JEWISH GOVERNMENT
TO THE ROMAN.

For centuries the Romans had pursued a policy of conquest, until in the days of Tiberius, according to the best authorities, the population of the Empire was about 120,000,- 000. " The subjugated countries that lay beyond the limits of Italy were designated provinces." In reconstructing a conquered territory, in respect to its legal and social life, the Romans "had the good sense to act in general, with prudence and mildness, having regard in their appointments to local peculiarities and existing institutions, so far as the intended adjunction to the Roman power permitted,in order to avoid giving the provincials provocation for opposing their new masters. Under ordinary circumstances, the government of the provinces was conducted by authorities sent for the purpose from Rome." "The pro-consuls, proprietors, and proprietorial lieutenants, when about to proceed into their several provinces, received instructions for their guidance from the Emperor; in cases in which they Avere found insufficient, they Avere to apply for special directions to the imperial head of the State." "There was also in the Senatorial provinces a procurator [this was Pilate's position], who raised the incomes intended, not for the treasury, but for the Emperor's privy purse; the smaller provinces, like Judea, which belonged to Syria, Avere altogether governed by such."

Criminal justice was wholly in the hands of the local governor, and extended not only over the provincals, but the Roman citizens as well; in important cases the Governors applied for a decision to the Emperor. As the Romans carefully abstained from making any changes in religious matters, so in Palestine the judging of crimes against religion was left by them to the high-priest and the Sanhedrim, even so far as condemnation to death; but the execution of the sentence depended on the procurator (Joseph. Antiq. xx : 9. 1; Mark xiv: 53, 55, 62, 65; John xviii: 31). The Jews at least during the time covered by the Gospels, enjoyed the free exercise of their religion. They had their synagogues or temples of public worship, where they served God without molestation, streaming thither at their great festivals from all parts of the land, and making what offerings or contributions they pleased."

"In order to enforce the taxes, and gene- rally aid the procurator, a body of Roman soldiers was put at his disposal, which had their quarters permanently in the country, their head station being at Cæsarea." "A portion of the troop was always stationed in Jerusalem at the Passover, in order to aid in preserving the peace [see page 59]. They had their quarters in the citadel Antonia. which commanded the temple, and so controlled the city. (Antiq. xix: 9.2; xx:4. 3; Acts xxi : 31. sq; xxii: 24; xxiii:23).

"The Romans and Jews first came into political relations about B. C. 161, when Judas Maccabæus, being moved by the great and widely spread military renown of the Romans, sent an embassy to Rome, and formed with them a treaty offensive and defensive, but with the special view of obtaining help against Demetrius, King of Syria, (I Mace. viii; Joseph. Antiq. xii: 10.6; Justin, xxvi : 3)."

Judea became a Roman province B. C. 63.

"The first procurator was Copinus; he was followed by Marcus Ambivius; then came Ammins Rufus, in whose time Augustus died, A. D. 14; the next was Valerius Gratus, who was appointed by Tiberius; he continued in the province eleven years, and was then succeeded by Pontius Pilate, whose government lasted ten years." (Kitto's Cyclopæd.. article Roman Empire).

TRADITIONAL SAYINGS OF CHRIST.

In connection with this passage of the Acta, it may be interesting to the reader to see some of the sayings attributed to our Savior by early writers, but unrecorded in. the Evangelists. One instance occurs in the New Testament, Acts xx : 35 : " Remember the words of the Lord Jesus, how he said, It is more blessed to give than to receive."

The following are given as specimens:

1. "He who longs to be rich is like a man who drinks sea-water; the more he drinks the more thirsty he becomes, and never leaves off drinking till he perishes."

2. " Pilate says to him, what is Truth? Jesus says, Truth is from Heaven. Pilate says, Is there not truth upon earth? Jesus says to Pilate, See how one who speaks the truth is judged by those who have power upon earth."

3. "On the same day, seeing one working on the Sabbath, he said to him, O man. if indeed thou knowest what thou doest, thou art blessed; but if thou knowest not, thou art accursed, and a transgressor of the law."

4. " He who is near me is near the fire; he who is far from me is far from the Kingdom."

5. " In whatsoever I may find you, in this will I also judge you."

6.   " Never be joyful except when ye shall look on your brother in love."

(Hoffman, Leben Jesu; also The Gospel according to the Hebrews, recovered, translated, annotated and analyzed by E. B. Nicholson, M. A., London, 1879).

(Note f, page 61.)

THE POWER OF LIFE AND DEATH.

"Although the Sanhedrim had passed their sentence, there remained a serious obstacle before it could be carried into execution. *On the contested point whether the Jews, under the Roman government, possessed the power of life and death, it is not easy to state the question with brevity and distinctness.* Notwithstanding the apparently clear and distinct recognition of the Sanhedrim, that they had not authority to put any man to death ; notwithstanding the remarkable concurrence of rabbinical tradition with this declaration, which asserts that the nation had been deprived of the power of life and death forty years before the destruction of the city. many of the most learned writers, some indeed of the ablest of the fathers, from arguments arising out of the practice of Roman provincial jurisprudence, and from later facts in the evangelic history and that of the Jews, have supposed that, even if, as is doubtful, they were deprived of this power in civil, they retained it in religious cases. Some have added, that even in the latter the ratification of the sentence by the Roman governor, or the permission to carry it into execution, was necessary. According to this view, the object of the Sanhedrim was to bring the case before Pilate as a civil charge ; since the assumption of a royal title and authority implied a design to cast off the Roman yoke. Or, if they retained the right of capital punishment in religious cases, it was contrary to usage, in the proceedings of the Sanhedrim, as sacred as law itself, to order an execution on the day of preparation for the Passover. As, then, they dared not violate that usage, and as delay was in every way dangerous, either from the fickleness of the people, who, having been momentarily wrought up to a pitch of deadly animosity against Jesus, might again, by some act of power or goodness on his part, be carried away back to his side; or in case of tumult, from the unsolicited intervention of the Romans, their plainest course was to obtain, if possible, the immediate support and assistance of the government.

"In my opinion, formed upon the study of the cotemporary Jewish history, the power of the Sanhedrim, at this period of political changes and confusion, on this, as well as on other points, was altogether undefined. Under the Asmonean princes, the sovereign, uniting with the civil and religious supremacy, the high-priesthood with the royal power, exercised, with the Sanhedrim as his council, the highest political and civil jurisdiction. Herod, whose authority depended upon the protection of Rome, and was maintained by his wealth, and in part by foreign mercenaries, although he might leave to the Sanhedrim, as the supreme tribunal, the judicial power, and, in ordinary religious cases, might admit their unlimited jurisdiction, yet no doubt watched and controlled their proceedings with the jealousy of an Asiatic despot, and practically, if not formally, subjected all their decrees to his revision : at least he would not have permitted any encroachment on his own supreme authority. In fact, according to the general tradition of the Jews, he at one time put to death the whole Sanhedrim : and since, as his life advanced, his tyranny became more watchful and suspicious, he was more likely to diminish than increase the powers of the national tribunal. In the short interval of little more than thirty years which had elapsed since the death of Herod, nearly ten had been occupied by the reign of Archelaus. On his deposal, the Sanhedrim had probably extended or resumed its original functions, but still the supreme civil authority rested in the Roman procurator. All the commotions excited by turbulent adventurers who infested the country, or by Judas the Galilean and his adherents, would fall under the cognizance of the civil governor, and were repressed by his direct interference. Nor can capital religious offences have been of frequent occurrence, since it is evident that the rigour of the Mosaic Law had been greatly relaxed, partly by the tendency of the age, which ran in a counter direction to those acts of idolatry against which the Mosaic statutes were chiefly framed, and left few crimes obnoxious to the extreme penalty. Nor, until the existence of their polity and religion was threatened, first by the progress of Christ, and afterward of his religion, would they have cared to be armed with an authority which it was rarely, if ever, necessary or expedient to put forth in its full force.

"This, then, may have been, strictly speaking, a new case, the first which had occurred since the reduction of Judea to a Roman province. The Sanhedrim, from whom all jurisdiction in political cases was withdrawn, and who had no recent precedent for the infliction of capital punishment on any religious charge, might think it more prudent (particularly during this hurried and tumultuous proceeding, which commenced at midnight, and must be dispatched with the least possible delay) at once to disclaim any authority which, however the Roman governor seemed to attribute to them, he might at least prevent their carrying into execution." (Milman, in his History of Christianity).

(Note g, page 62.)

CLAUDIA PROCULA, THE WIFE OF PILATE.

"From Matt. xxvii:19, it appears that Pilate had his wife (named probably Proda, or Claudia Procula) with him. A partial knowledge of Itoman history might lead the reader to question the historic credibility of Matthew in this particular. In the earlier periods, and, indeed, so long as the commonwealth subsisted, it was very unusual for the governors of provinces to take their wives with them (Senec. De Controv. 25), and in the strict regulations which Augustus introduced he did not allow the favor except in peculiar and specified cases (Sueton. Aug. 24). The practice however grew to be more and more prevalent, and was (says Winer, Real-wort, in 'Pilate') customary in Pilate's time.

"It is evident from Tacitus, that at the time of the death of Augustus, Germaniens had his wife, Agrippina, with him in Germany (Annal. i: 40. 41; comp, iii: 33. 59; Joseph. Antiq. xx: 10. 1; Ulpian. iv:2). Indeed, in the beginning of the reign of Tiberius, Germanicus took his wife with him into the East. Piso, the prefect of Syria, took his wife also along with him at the same time (Tacit. Annal, ii: 54. 55). ' But,' says Lardner (i:152), 'nothing can render this (the practice in question) more apparent than a motion made in the Roman senate by Severus Cæsena, in the fourth consulship of Tiberius, and second of Drusus Cæsar (A. D. 21), that no magistrate to whom any province was assigned, should be accompanied by his wife, except the Senate's rejecting it, and that with some indignation' (Tacit. Annal, iii: 33. 34). The fact mentioned incidently, or rather implied, in Matthew, being thus confirmed by full and unquestionable evidence, cannot fail to serve as a corroboration of the evangelical history." (Kitto's Bib. Lit.)

"It is a remarkable fact that a heathen woman had the courage to plead the cause of our Saviour when his own disciples forsook him, and when the Jewish people and authorities thirsted for his innocent blood. It is equally remarkable that she and her weak husband, clothed with the authority of the Roman law and justice, should characterize the condemned Jesus as that just man. The student of the unconscious prophecies of heathenism will naturally connect this expression with the famous passage in Plato's ' Republic,' where the great sage of Greece describes the ideal of a just man as one who, without doing any wrong, may assume the appearance of the grossest injustice; yea, who shall be scourged, tortured, fettered, deprived of his eyes, and, after having endured all possible sufferings, fastened to a post, and must restore again the beginning and prototype of righteousness." (Plato's Works, vol. IV, p. 78, sqq. ed. Ast. p. 360. E. ed. Bip).

"Aristotle also says of the perfectly just man, ' that he stands far above the political order and constitution as it exists; that he must break it wherever he appears.' The prophecies of Greek wisdom, and the majesty of the Boman law, here unite in a Boman body, the wife of the imperial representative at Jerusalem, to testify to the innocence and righteousness of Christ in the darkest hour of his trial before wicked men. She was probably a proselyte of the gate, or one of those God-fearing heathen, who, without embracing the Jewish religion, were longing and groping in the dark after 'the unknown God.'" (From Dr. Shaff's additions to Lange on Matthew, p. 511).

(Note h, page 63.)

GEMONIÆ.

This expression is equivalent to : "You are in danger of doing what will seriously reflect upon Cæsar." The word is used in Val. Max. 6. 9; Liv. 38. 59; Suct. Tib. 53. 61; Tacit. Hist. iii: 74. According to Anthon, the *Gemoniæ scales* were steps at Rome, near the prison of Tullianum, down which the bodies of those who had been executed in prison were thrown into the Forum, to be exposed to the gaze of the multitude.

(Note i, page 64.)

THE HAND-WASHING.

"Attracted towards the court by this shout, ' No king but Cæsar,' we find the judge just in the act of yielding, under the popular cry, ' If thou let this man go, thou art not Cæsar's friend;' for he dreads the utterance of such a charge, however absurd, in the ears of the irritable Tiberius, his master. Therefore he gives sentence as they demand; but 'he took water and washed his hands before the multitude saying, I am innocent of the blood of this just person.'

"Singular paradox; a magistrate innocent of the blood of one whom judicially he murders, while declaring him just in the same breath! No, no! Pilate, think not with water to wash off that stain of blood from thy hands. For, falling upon the official hand that pretends to weigh justice in the balance, its stain hath struck too deep for any water cleansing. "The untitled, powerless, private man, forced by the mob to deeds of cruelty, might perhaps with the tears of ingenuous sorrow wash out the blood spot ! But thou art imperial Cæsar's legate, Pilate. Thine is the strong arm of the law, flashing its gleaming sword, by God's ordinance, in the defence of innocence, as well as in vengence on guilt. Thy gorgeous ermine is full wide to shelter in its ample folds this torn and bleeding lamb that the fierce dogs of bigotry are thus savagely pursuing. With all thy pompous pretence to dignity and chivalrous Homan honour, thou art but a miserable pedlar in blood ! Baser than Judas whose narrow soul thought thirty pieces of silver a worthy price, thou art selling him over again for a worthless smile from these ecclesiastical bloodhounds, whom every manly instinct of thy nature loathes and abhors! Thou art a poor coward, Pilate, that thou fearest such a mob, with the strong arm of Cæsar to defend thee, and the broad shield of eternal justice to hold before thee. No, Pilate, no! Not all the waters of Jordan that washed leprous Naaman clean; not all the waters that ever gushed from the rills of Siloam ; not all the tears of sorrow that shall flow through eternity for thy sin, shall ever wash off that stain of blood!

"Yet how common seems this mistake of Pilate, that the unrighteous judgement of an official, given under pressure of strong temptations from personal consideration, — either of desire to win popular favor; or avaricious hankering after gain; or the impulse of partisan malice or party obligations may be atoned for, by giving the innocent the benefit of one's personal convictions and professions as an offset against the damage to him of one's villainous official deed; and that it is enough to perform a little penitential handwashing for the filthy job done to popular order! How little do men seem to comprehend the solemn truth, that, as in the Church, under his revealed law, God hath appointed his ministers to be his representatives, and will surely punish the corrupt and unfaithful servants, so in the state, under that natural law which he hath revealed to all men alike. 'The powers that be are ordained of God;' and will likewise be held accountable to God. "That the magistrate, called by the public voice to office, is in his sphere, The minister of God for good,' to the upright citizen, and the minister of God, 'a revenger to execute wrath upon him that doeth evil.' And every curse threatened against official unfaithfulness in the Church, lies with all its force,in the other sphere also, against the magistrate who misrepresents and caricatures God's essential justice. Ye cowardly handwashers! If ye have not the manly courage to breast the billows of popular fury,and make your official voice heard above all the howls of the mob, then why thrust yourselves into places to which, obviously God hath not called you? If Tiberius, moved by the popular clamor, threaten you, then tell Tiberius and the mob, 'we ought to obey God rather than men,' and go into exile with a clear conscience for your companion. To the sort of men whom God calls to represent him, the passion of Tiberius and the curses of the mob are sweet music compared with the accusings of conscience! Beware how ye make light of bartering justice, either for the popular smile, or for place, or for gold. If by a righteous Providence ye be not driven to Pilate's doom of exile, and suicide, like Judas; yet, be assured that, amid the curses of the ruined, the Avails of the heart-broken and the moans of the murdered ringing in your ears, ye shall wash, and wash in vain at that blood-spot throughout eternity !

"And, on the other hand, when public virtue hath come to such a pass, that the clamor of the mob, instead of the covenanted law, must find utterance through Pilate on the bench; or, that popular sentiment regards Pilate's use of his official authority for personal ends, either of avarice, ambition or passion, as a venial sin of natural infirmity, that a little hand-washing may atone for; then may we know that the day of political doom is nigh such a people, even at their doors; for now, 'judgement lingereth not and damnation slumbereth not.' The judgment on such a people hath in fact already begun." (From Dr. Stuart Robinson's eloquent Discourses of Redemption. D. Appleton & Co., N. Y., 1866).

(Note k, page 66.)

DIONYSIUS.

During the night following the day the Crucifixion of Jesus took place, Pilate sent a brief account of what had occurred to the Emperor, as he himself states (see page 68). The Acta was not written until some months afterwards. The turbulence of the Jews continued — the beginnings no doubt of the great rebellion which, in the days of Titus, led to the destruction of their capital and the dispersion of the nation. From the book of Acts in the New Testament, we learn that the preaching of the Apostles excited great and general attention, and afforded occasion for repeated attacks upon them by the Pharisees and Sadducees. Amid these turmoils Pilate trembled for his own position, and wrote this detailed and full communication to Tiberius in order to set himself right with the authorities at Rome, (see p. 35, 5).

During the interim between the first and second writing, a period probably of five or six months, the events of our Savior's life, teachings, miracles, persecution, crucifixion, resurrection and ascension, had excited intense interest throughout the entire East, and thousands of converts to Christianity had been made.

The Dionysius here alluded to was a heathen philosopher from Athens, who was at this time in Heliopolis in Egypt. There he beheld that remarkable eclipse of the sun, as he termed it, which took place at the death of Christ, and exclaimed to his friend Appolophanes, " Either the Divinity suffers or sympathizes with some sufferer."

In that day there was a military road, which had been built by the Romans, extending from the principal cities of Egypt to Jerusalem, the course of which is to-day marked by Telegraph posts, crossing the present Suez Canal at the small Arab village of Kantara, near the lake Menzaleh.

It is not at all to be wondered at, that such a singular saying of a great and learned man should soon have become generally known in all that region; and it is not strange that Pilate should quote this to Tiberius, to give the greater weight to his representations.

(Note 1. page 66.)

THE FIRST HOUR.

"To wards the first hour of the night I threw my mantle around me, and went down into the city , towards the gates of Golgotha," i. e. *at seven o'clock P. M.* This passage of the Acta gives wonderful vividness to the description, and shows the uneasiness and remorse that already filled Pilate's mind, in view of the events of that terrible day.

FINIS.

www.ingramcontent.com/pod-product-compliance
Lightning Source LLC
Chambersburg PA
CBHW071632040426
42452CB00009B/1583